MW01274726

PRAISE FOR *rump + flank*

"Years of personal and poetic experience have been consolidated in Carol Harvey Steski's marvellous collection *rump + flank*. Agile, with a flowing immediacy to the language, these poems are richly inventive and resonant. This is a visceral, sometimes raw, book with hidden time bombs just beneath the surface. Harvey Steski's voice is unique and superbly confident, speaking with a fluent urgency. It's a book I've been anticipating for years."

Patrick Friesen
AUTHOR OF
Outlasting the Weather: Selected & New Poems 1994–2020

"Cutting, sharp and sonically rich, the poems in *rump + flank* dazzle with rhythm, image and meaning. Open and compact they 'break apart + enter' with verve and skill. A playful confidence shakes and shimmers 'with one fell swoop/+ last gasp relieved' so readers are 'swallowed wave after wave.' Subject matter, often rooted in the body, includes the personality behind typeface and a cancerous growth named Clog. An accomplished debut."

Catherine Graham
AUTHOR OF
The Celery Forest and *Aether: An Out-of-Body Lyric*

rump

flank

rump

+

flank

carol harvey steski

NeWest Press

COPYRIGHT © CAROL HARVEY STESKI 2021

All rights reserved. The use of any part of this publication —
reproduced, transmitted in any form or by any means, electronic,
mechanical, recording or otherwise, or stored in a retrieval system —
without the prior consent of the publisher is an infringement of the
copyright law. In the case of photocopying or other reprographic
copying of the material, a licence must be obtained from Access
Copyright before proceeding.

Library and Archives Canada Cataloguing in Publication
Title: Rump + flank : poems / Carol Harvey Steski.
Other titles: Rump and flank | Rump plus flank
Names: Steski, Carol Harvey, author.
Description: Series statement: Crow said poetry | Poems.
Identifiers: Canadiana (print) 20200403923 |
Canadiana (ebook) 20200403958 | ISBN 9781774390283 (softcover) |
ISBN 9781774390290 (epub)
Classification: LCC PS8637.T48395 R86 2021 | DDC C811/.6—dc23

Board editor: Doug Barbour
Book design: Natalie Olsen, Kisscut Design
Cover photo: © Carmen Palma / Stocksy.com
Author photo: Anil Mungal

NeWest Press acknowledges the Canada Council for the Arts, the
Alberta Foundation for the Arts, and the Edmonton Arts Council for
support of our publishing program. This project is funded in part
by the Government of Canada. ¶ NeWest Press acknowledges that
the land on which we operate is Treaty 6 territory and a traditional
meeting ground and home for many Indigenous Peoples, including
Cree, Saulteaux, Niitsitapi (Blackfoot), Métis, and Nakota Sioux.

#201, 8540–109 Street Edmonton, Alberta T6G 1E6
780.432.9427
NEWEST PRESS www.newestpress.com

No bison were harmed in the making of this book.
Printed and bound in Canada   1 2 3 4 5   23 22 21

For my family, in gratitude

contents

rump + flank

I

various cuts

various cuts

she is rump + flank
she is side + swivel hip
twirling skirtsteak chopsmack
+ tender in the loins   she is
bonein she is marrowsoft
+ babyback with lilylivered
open eyes of round   she is

all ribs all tongue
tips + shoulder blades
+ wings made of fascia,
flayed

red tide

this florida day, a pleasant oven
with its blue door cracked
mirage escapes   hovering
at the junction
between sea + sky
sand is warmed glass

hermit crabs gather
at rare hot tub parties
with the neighbours
chat up new real estate ventures,
eyeing the right time to flip:
this niche a seller's market
despite the downturn

abandoned beach
the smell of mass murder slaps us in the face
red tide has blossomed
in the long throats of ocean locals
+ quietly choked each one
off, gill by poisoned gill,
there, there
shhhh

evicted carcasses   scattered
like blown-out tires along the tamiami
various phases of decay
displayed + baking here:
bone racks + bloated bellies
cheek holes + fins

before our eyes
the nightmare spreads —
becomes the feasting seagulls' —
a time bomb of a fish fry
not enough skin left on this carnage
to hold even one last
dying wish

starfish

an unclenched fist
she is placid as saline, stoic

as a pinwheel on a windless day
the sea star lays down

on the broken homes
of rubbled shells, spreads her

nippled limbs like an outstretching
yawn

she bides her time on the bed, the floor,
a vertical face

anywhere she is flung   she's stuck
a silent high-five

oyster night

You were culled just for me,
a plump tongue shucked
upon the half-shell   a whole note dropped
headlong into the bleak song
you were born to sing.

Your eagerness to please people is legendary
generations of necks decorated
with the by-products
of your chronic irritation,
      a quiet, iridescent despair.

If that weren't enough service
you compel us to covet the salty bodies
of neighbours + strangers
      (or, at least to flicker interest
in our own bored relationships).

I don't need a mignonette
or hot-sauce costume,
just your fresh press against me
      mouth to mouth
silk muscling silk.

With one fell swoop

                + last gasp relieved

you're swallowed
wave after wave
back to sea.

chewing glass, two takes

1 : liquid

open your mouth
molten orbs bubble
like chewing gum,
feel the skin release
its curve against the tonguetip
every breath rounding, *oh*
   oh

in the last gassy chaw + blow,
science with its cold-pressed facts
meets the hot swagger of art,
you see your funhouse face in the result:
all its wobbling, iridescent
splendour

2 : solid

there would. be. blood.
sudden jaw. wired.
  shut.
            crush
       +
  grind.

pulverized ideas. thrust.

back. to their carbon.
starting point.   on that trembling. lip.

of a big.

    bang.

pre-conceived. before you even knew.
you wanted this.
        + *ohgod.*

how.
    you. wanted.

this.

metamorphosis

Turn up the heat.
Sweat sugar through the skin.
Pores blow open,
metamorphosis begins.
Catharsis in shaking up the agenda.

My life is in this pan.
A tumble of roots + tubers.
Like abandoned landmines
these secret ambitions
spent years in the wordless dirt learning
to keep their mouths shut.

Itchy in the way of last-ditch efforts
they shimmied up like slivers
+ spread before the world.
Now, exposed to flames
my brown-bit dreams
sear fast to the pan's enamel,
the inferno's glow.

I scrape them all up   sticky + glittering
fork-tender stars
I can break apart
+ enter.

pitting cherries

Skulls choke the drain, dumped
here like a yardful of unmarked graves.
Mama's kitchen sink
a stainless-steel killing field.

Her Scorsese-style weapon   a cross
between ball-peen hammer + nail gun
delivers efficient pointblank trauma:

>   quickhit to the head
>   instant redvelvet spray.

With springshot cocked + loaded
her itchy triggerfinger trips
another bluntforce nutshot
+ the stress released
is like a firing-range fantasy   or orgasm,

>   burst apart.

>   She revels

in the abattoir she herself conceived,
this crime scene for a greater good
with its cherryspatter high.

Then roams the hallways for days,
fingerprints + conscience stained
the shade of latent rage.

duck fat

like drinking quicksilver
but innocent as milk
or melted silk
sweet yet sheer, caramel
without the muffling clutch
on the heart

coats like molten candle wax
over my throat, glosses
my thumbs   my fingers
+ as I lick at them   lick

at them
my tongue teethes,
becomes a cat's, skins off
this starched surface of gold
in an obsessive shred,
needs more

ladies: this could be it!
finally, a lip smacking incentive
to sweeten the pot, put that smile
on your man's face,
a reason to swallow
again

+ again

mammatus clouds

The name mammatus *is derived from the Latin* mamma,
meaning udder or breast.
— WIKIPEDIA

The mammatus clouds
bubble + sag,
full breasts pulled south
by the weight of mouths,
a latched litter of kittens
straining all resources.

Glands engorged
as water balloons hanging
from gravity's fists,
anticipation building.
Or bagged milk,
those plastic pouches brimming
before the triangle tip is snipped
to release the flow. As a girl
I used to hold them in my arms
like wobbling babies,
cradling a dream.

Wait: the let-down is imminent
triggered by infants' instinct
who knew, the strength of their pull?
Small tongues muscling the song
from the instrument
with perfect urgent embouchures,
that voracious art of knowing
what lies beyond the flesh
to harvest what you need.

resurrection

This campfire throws
so much heat I wince

                              yet move in closer
moth-drawn
to Northern Ontario
stereotypes.

Here the dead are reborn as heroes:
fallen logs + saved trash
        crackling + sparking
expired lives resurrected, repurposed
to the short-term service of others.

Honouring their cause, I roast marshmallows.
This craft demands a steady hand:
undercooking leaves the dusty skin intact
but if caught ablaze, a brittle crust
scatters ashes in your mouth like a black blizzard.

I need the slow reveal,
a cascading flush—
like when you finally understood
what all your secret parts were made for—
that deepens into a soft buckling of knees.

Inspired into active duty now,
I step into the flames. Against a backdrop
of frying stars, my body thrums,
emits tremendous love
as I render.

veronica lake

sixty mile-an-hour wind
nipples whitecaps into a chilled pluck,
the lakeskin whipped
to stiff peaks

every lick
of the shoreline
rips another grain from me,
how much more can i take?   i moan

like a 1940s icon
      upper lip stiff as driftwood
in the face of lurching
change

the waitress

This iconic Canadiana resort camp
sports on its logged walls
a circus of varnished fish
in various stages of gape.
The lone evening-shift waitress
attends school during the days,
keeps a toddler back home.
On smoking summer nights
she dishes deep-fried dreams
to fishermen + families
before the bonfires raze, blurring
the line where horizon
+ flame converge
in a hazy lick.

The smell of the grease trap
is saunaed into every part of her —
a signature scent —
+ even her ex-lover
three years removed
tastes salt + creamed oil
on his thick fingers still,
+ thinks
of her.

curmudgeon

Half-submerged in the algae sluice
like a greasy green egg, sunny side
greeting the day with a grudge,
this bullfrog is thick
as a grown man's fist

+ Tony-Soprano-tough.
His whole body's an open mouth
flipped inside out. All day he waits,
self-basting + belching glottal stops
uncontested: a drunkard's dream.

He lives in a perennial meat-sweat.
Only moves as extreme need arises
+ then, at a rubber-snail's pace,
fat elastic joints + beefy limbs
yawning.

Even when that ancient urge stirs
wet in down-below folds,
he just lies right back + snaps
a band of fingers to summon
his infinity from the reeds.

tweenage wasteland

The lake this year is choked with tadpoles,
everything cycling back.
Pollywogs, those prepubescent frogs,
someday they'll grunt nervously
at dance parties, but for now
these half-legged, half-flippered
amphibian wannabes
are reminders of impotent youth,
precursor to full-blown
angst.

Last night's dream was wet
+ webbed, my throat
so coated with warts
that I could hardly swallow
a fly.

canuck problems

tonguetied to a frozen pole
    the stick of hot skin   steam rises
pale pink to white
off this fried-ice nightmare

you can't run from your urges
especially now   sealed
politely as you are
to this pain

cells that should be dead
still emote like smouldering loins
shed old stories of other
stupid shit we've done

shark teeth

At the beach we sit on grins,
with our sandpaper bottoms
polishing overbites to glass
+ try to imagine
how these pearly blacks came to be here
once shed from ancient mouths
        un-locked + un-loaded
from mechanical jawbones,
rendered effectively inert.

Thousands of choppers
lost in a single lifetime   one by one
dislodged   replaced
dislodged   replaced
a round-the-clock enamel factory
of Henry-Ford-esque efficiency.

What became of those assembly line by-products?
Did lateral cusplets + serrations drift listlessly
through millennia   floating alongside
the flotsam + jetsam of sea junk
+ jellyfish schools?
Surf relentless swells + curls
riding centuries of big rollers
before finally being spit out   petrified
on this shore?

I pity the tooth fairy,
having neither the time nor the means
to deliver whatever currency
this vast collection might fetch.
Nor the opportunity, really, as these fish
don't stop for sleep.
Instead they chase down wakes
in concentric circles, swirling.

Haunted by chronic loss,
they harbour the common knowledge of neurotics:
that eventually all our lovers run away.
Even our own body parts
abandon ship on the regular.

.

mosquito breeding ground

rain has not given up the ghost
this spring, our puppy hopes
soaked to a heavy-
headed sag

we watch divots in the city's skin
fill with our tears, laying
layers of wet bedding
for the nurseries

soon, cesspool-wombs
bloat with embryos, new souls afloat
on rafts of foam   spanning worlds
dreaming the same red stain

* * *

emerging fresh from the gauze,
high-pressured wannabe moms
know the drill   take to the air
with tool belts + sensibilities strapped

while the males flit from lily to lily
chasing infinity, oblivious
to nature's countdown on
their ephemeral heads

* * *

evening fields of green wheat
breathe a sigh of relief
at the wide sky's finally
evolved palette

in a man-made crop circle
two lovers slap bugs off each others' asses
    interrupting the needleflow
they itch + curse

at the damage done
in bumps + blood drawn
the flush of fast sex
siphoned from their cheeks

complexions drained to a zombie pallor
that even the setting sun's bronze cast
can't warm back up
to human

cousins

gourds flourish today
chinese bottles, crowns of thorn
polished dolls for the mantel
these ornamental debutantes
     skim across my hearth
insulated in frivolity,
show dogs bred for good behaviour

while their pumpkin cousins,
harbingers of thinning light,
are assigned a different lot   hunted for sport
they know their days are numbered
in slits + basic shapes,
+ their end will come in smoke

what else to do but live like thieves,
sputtering wreckage
comparing scars?

     + then
as the heavy snow whorls
these homeless folk   burn out alone

on steps all over suburbia

pumpkin farm

Stubble smoke smudges the air
from nearby farmers' fields.
Thousands of pumpkins tremble together
on the greenhouse slab,
a rite of passage no ancestor has escaped.

Puttied terracotta, blood-orange, crusted
with mud, they've been cut
from their soiled beds.
No role now but to dazzle me
+ sacrifice themselves
to Halloween knives.

Worthy squash: rotund or squat,
lopsided or long like Bert,
millions of faces carve themselves
as I pass by.

Sherbet flesh—sinewy + smelling of
raw crotch—lines the cut smiles
+ eyeholes, brows,
the triangle noses.

Imagine candles lit inside
singeing the meat   the way the thought of hot sex

burns you up
sometimes.

plum creek

plum creek sounds like a place i'd like to see

where mottled clouds congeal over
thickly knitted woods, wool weaving
moss in the rocks + crannies
lichen clinging for its life to stumps

where the mushrooms puff + blush
a thousand different shades of bark
even plug-in to neon generators
+ light up the forest floor:
organic patio lanterns

+ then, the plums

millions packed tight filling the creekbed
like a vein or a bathtub full of murk
grinding along, skinning themselves
on the way to jars, where bunches of
women wait patiently with
bare feet, twitching toes

what is it about this name, how it rolls
off teeth + rounds my lips,
its colour bleeding into the eyes,
essence busting its way up the nose
how i can hold these words in my hand,
plum-smooth skin pressing mine

snowball

for Laura

at the saints roller rink
it all went down in snowballs
+ *heart of glass*
pump-pumping
aerodynamic
around the corners
disco moons
splashing
ambient dusk
precision beads
absorbing
the quiet shock
boys + girls
pulled by friday night's
centrifugal force
holding tender
hands slender hips
swivelling in rhythm
on the slick track
rubber wheels
locked eyes

truth or dare?

The day the girl posed this to her best friend,
a textbook summer scorcher.
Their lungs were boiled perogies
protected by gauzy cotton tank tops,
+ freckles that had tiptoed years earlier onto
exposed shoulders + other sunny places
today were dark + frantic.

Everything seemed affected.

Crickets stopped hopscotching the chalkboards with their nails,
too tired or finally bored with the Prairies.
Tar bubbled in the streets' grids
threatening the stability of the fault lines
in the same way ratcheting gas prices
jeopardized the lead-heavy 70s.
A watering ban left its yellow brand
on lawns though the marigolds,
always composed,
snuck sips when no one was looking.

But nothing could placate that sky.

All afternoon cumulonimbus clouds
advanced the plot on a stop-motion horizon
(only things around still moving by now)
foreshadowed looming teenage years,
those duelling themes of relief + dread
blooming to a head.

Dare, she whispered.

angel food cake

you spent every
childhood birthday
at this cherry mouth
of memory

    angel food

the very name
conjuring mystique

communion
of your young life's occasions
its sponge dissolved
like a salve
on your tongue
+ you wondered,

     am   i

       an angel,

then?

when children loved vegetables

when their feet were bare
rough from days of running
on sun-cracked ground
        the mud clumped
over toes as they
wandered through watered gardens
pulling sweet carrots
from their homes
        tossing lace tops to the wind
unthreading peas
+ stopping beans
like snakes across
the earth   + remember
at the end of it all?
crisp stalks of rhubarb
(leaves big as me)
dipping into bowls
of white sugar, eyes
+ crystal mouths
pinched tight
as the tongues sour

toddlerhood
(or, if *sesame street*'s don music were a dad)

night night
+ the whole world crumples
in a culmination of injustices
pint-sized, but real:

    snack-fails
    unwanted grooming
    conspiracies of mislaid plush-stuffies

                         flick-flick-flick our flayed nerves

to the edge, crescendo
to a collective hairy conniption
of *don music* proportions

+ at the apex
we slam the ivories
with our sweet-potato heads

the buzzer

Kawhi Leonard's miracle shot sends Toronto Raptors into Game 7 elation —
Thanks to a shot that bounced three times and dropped as time expired,
the Raptors advance to the NBA's final four with a 92-90 win.
— NATIONAL POST, MAY 13, 2019

The buzzer began its proclamation
a dissertation on closure,
taking the full allotment of time
to reach the point   when out of the clear sky

burning orange like an asteroid
crashing the atmosphere's lip,
a rimshot caught in the frozen throat
of a northern nation.

In that instant various gods were called upon
to wield their concurrent powers,
an intervention to tip the balance
common resolve for a small-m miracle.

Then, despite conflicting belief systems
+ historically warring orthodoxies
the disparate prayers
of the multi-faithed were —

mysteriously + smashing
all reasonable odds —
answered   in holy sequence
like a threefold benediction:

one
for each
bounce.

praise

imagine field of sunflowers
straight-spined host of angels
singing loud
mOuths wide
with glory
flaming halo-frames

a gospel choir
swaying far + wide
leaves in the air

hallelujah
shining down

II

typefacing

Allow the face to speak in its natural idiom.

THE ELEMENTS OF TYPOGRAPHIC STYLE
BY ROBERT BRINGHURST

times new roman

Font of Law. Government Type-Speak,
Bureaucratic Prattle.   Its serifs
stand on guard for thee; stiff
as billy clubs they fall
in line, one after another
+ another.

This typeface sets
down rules in bone   in carbon-
dated dust   an iron-clad
handshake on paper,
the real deal.

Its serious business dictates behaviour.
Mandates are rigid   cocked
+ loaded for discharge,
the legal team's review
poised for public scrutiny.

Politicians bow
at the foot of this font,
live + die
by its sword of promises.

Voters, too, seem to trust these characters
these barbed weapons that,
    more often than not,
are swallowed down
as truth.

arial

relieved of tails i'm pinched clean
+   as my name suggests
blown hot-full
          as balloons in a blank room
or molten glass bloated
into iridescent bubbles

orb: polar opposite of hole
i'm a carbon-dioxide junkie
let me float your ideas one to next
without passing judgment
like cumulus clouds
                              shrugging shoulders loose

released

          unleashed   UP
                                              +
                                   uP
                    up   +

comic sans

You're off-kilter,
I know the kind.
Manic clown, you freak me out.
You'd gnaw the head off a raw rubber chicken
if you had the chance.
Can't be trusted,
your toothy cartoon chuckles
echo for miles.

Even the kids can't stand you now.
They'd like to shoot
the homemade cliché of you
through the barrel of a cannon,
paper every lamppost
with your ashes
widely publicizing your demise.

Like, die.

mistral

oh whisk me away,
sailing on your whimsy
right back to the 90s
to the French countryside
we are all crazy here
                    painting selfies
+ your breath
on my back
is hot + erotic
+ the fields
are a study
in yellow perfection
you're the crows
scratching frantic messages
onto the sky
you're a postcard
                    + everywhere i turn
another fucking
flash

courier

[INT. — DAY]

the old-school
film editor
is a romantic

    + a liar

raw footage
cannot reflect
the perfection
in his head, so

                    at odd
        angles two

sides of
the same
frame are
snipped

           re-
           sequenced
then

scotch-bound
firmly
in place
to stitch
a new truth

+ the remnants
of his own
cut-up
flaws
applaud
the floor

[FADES]

III

scar

scar

how to pinpoint
this scar   this cut mouth
paring knife frown
hoping against hope your blood
contains the dormant words
inside you

such release

a thin slice might bring
the litany of dichotomies
your life has been: one who kills
but yearns for birth

pushing
pushing through
the years

mis.carry (baby.b)

                              Interrupted
in your tracks.
       Auto-shutdown. Glottal

stop.

I don't have to eat you by mouth
to hide your scented evidence from predators.
Nature spared us that. I prepare
a pillow for your budded skull
on my comfortable lap of lymph + blood,
wait for nap-time to absorb your frozen
beats + bars,
                         your paused parts.

A mother's unconscious job:
the way a scavenger is programmed to pick
         with surgical precision
a fallen body clean.
(But my work comes with a sky full of love
+ too much grief to name.)

This soft labour complete,
the extinguished smoke of you
is burned like a woodcut
on my amygdala, hollow relief. So it goes,
the body a fracked landscape
fraught with probable
catastrophe.

Cue the reboot.
                         Jump-
       start. My faltering

heart.

coming of age

Pole to pole, fresh energy fries
as electric grid trips across the kilo-miles
dishing power to the people
in a succession of microscopic flint strikes,
shocked atoms spraying the stars
as they burn.

We barrel down the backroads
of the backwoods
of nowhere, Northern Ontario,
leave the future behind in a wake of sparks
for balding + thinning towns littered
with gasping 60s bungalows,
those short-sighted minimalist trims
+ miniature windows pinched tight,
smoked curtains closed
to keep progress at bay.

We plug into desolate
teenaged souls bored dim
in subterranean rec rooms.
Cultivating grown-up hips
+ thoughts, long limbs fumble
against the chesterfield's tweed,
generating static in high-fidelity cling.

The kids can't conserve these urges,
can't resist this essential service
they provide to each other —
    + the community-at-large —
like a local utility mainlining hope
against the blackouts

                    rolling in   rolling in

on one more infinite
night.

concussed

what i remember
the night i fell

smell of hockey jocks
+ crushed cigarettes

frozen concrete
brown thud

three-year-old brain
soft as foie gras

unchained
by a graceless freefall

through space
+ time

while grown-ups watched
the opposition score

＊ ＊ ＊

open car window
vomit sparkled the air

cold lights of a hospital room
mint kidney pan

years later i read
how such violence

to a mind so tender
sparks

undercurrents
of rage

trickle-to-trainwreck
no outlet

for the jangled disarray
+ fray of nerves

(in a ginger, to boot
my bedroom door

was a constant smash)
in precise hindsight

my parents' frustration
made sense

three souls
to keep afloat

+ disappointing
role models

in their own dearly departed
or vanished folks

garbage strike

I remember when the Big Smoke roasted
in its own refuse.
For thirty-nine raging days
a frivolous perk for workers
held us hostage-by-hotbox
until we all sold out.

                                        I loved you more then
before the trash canisters lurched,
purging-fantastic on their own delights
like binged-out trick-or-treaters
licking one-night fingers.

Under a tightening lid of clouds
the summer stewed + it didn't take long
for newly makeshift collection stations to fester.
Playgrounds repurposed for death
became a headlong flush down a plugged toilet
as the public's leftovers plunged
into a battle of brands: *no name* macaroni
elbowing highbrow-grocery T-bones
in a grassroots movement, an urban slurry.

                                        The air soured on many levels
while at home, eggshells shattered
even faster under our feet.

As the city rotted into Armageddon
politicians fiddled their then-Twitterless thumbs
+ citizens adapted like placid scavengers:
walking commuters scuttled underground
to shallow-breathe the somehow cleaner fumes
of subway culture while the rest of us   above the fold
spied, red-eyed, our last meals steaming
on every corner.

Eventually the standoff ended in concessions
(even civic inertia has its limits)
+ table scraps evaporated
from greenspaces for good.

But we were changed, you + I,
with the voters, all captured
in the plastic trap of apathy,
its walls too tall + rhetoric too slick,
to scale.

                                    See how indifference ferments

under the skin?
Five years later, a latent singe:
all smoulder + smoke
with no reasonable
way out.

timber

The woodsman's on a mission,
fells a big one today.
Watches sixty feet topple
like a knocked chopstick,
makes it look easy.
He digests the timber
slowly over several hours,
wearing it down
as a snake would its last meal.

Chunks it first
into parts the length of a full leg,
then again into shins. One by one
each stump is turned on its fresh wound.
The axe descends again in a tidy line,
cleaving each moment into a clean split,
the crack of before + after,
that splintering difference
between an open door
+ a door slammed shut.
Two neat worlds: a wife,

a wife   gone.

the art of communicating to males

I peel sticky notes from my tongue
+ hand them to you,
messages as direct + memorable
as a slapshot to the nuts.
But you're distracted
+ don't receive them,
repel them almost,
as if lint has gathered on the tacky strip.

They flutter, unheard, to the ground
so I speak more slowly
in grand, scotch-assisted charades.
You could be a brain surgeon
from another mother tongue
poised to crack my skull next,
but I dial up my volume louder
treating you as deaf, or dim-witted:

> Black sharpie block letters on white paper.
> Border of parading ants.
> Technicolor blinks.

 — Nothing.

New tactic: I. Pulse. Out. Morse. Code.
In. Hipthrusts.

Ah, now. You understand.

repressed

a swollen heart creaming
the latte's head: this
is *la barista's* love letter

unable to reveal her yearn
to his face, each day she kisses
pouting lips
after budding rose
after spreading fernfrond

onto the mugs
of hundreds
of strangers

rift

This collection of stilled limbs twists
into a random heap under hot sheets of night.
The scene is a snapshot: frozen
but for the rise

+ fall of breasts,
small intimacies of the breath:
on the inside, bladders of wind
    heave in
               blow out
    heave again
in that semi-automatic habit of life,

fan the invisible ire of our words
the last difference of opinion
that drove us here,
   facing walls.

coffee shop, southwest florida

1

These aging faces of Naples melt
in a sad denial of the facts,
decade after decade grasping for the past.
Eventually a circus of artists
was enlisted to stipple frescoes
over a lifetime of expensive
+ publicly accepted addictions.

See what their money buys them now:
canvas stretched to a high-pitched scream,
eyelids fused to skullsockets,
plastic buried as subterranean trash.

They're a wax parade masqueraded
as an everyday occasion,
desperation smouldering
beneath a golden Florida glow.

2

Cautiously we float this effigy of a man
through the slackjaw of the glass jar,
draw him from the chemical bath
preserved + inert
smelling of neither life nor death
spring nor fall.

Not a facial-hair follicle nor
sweat gland to be found
he's smooth as an ancient baby.
A waxed + effeminate version
of his great-grandfather, he betrays
the rugged hew of his family's males,
their swaggering dicks.

John Wayne bitchslaps shadows in his grave.

3

Happy couple in matching track suits + sneaks,
their eyes bulge lovingly
over mugs of decaf
+ gluten-free crumbs,
reusable water bottles primed
for the power-walk back
to the parking lot Jag.

They find romance
in his + hers nips + tucks,
jack + jill expressions
stitched in place
stamped to the past
like fossils to graves.

On Sundays they leave
their falsified bodies
as burnt offerings
at the alter of Ego.
Fooling no one,
no god.

skinner's box

A clatter of rib-bones,
like wind chimes constructed of wood
+ somehow less annoying.   Caged
the soft meatfist
is restrained from that urge
to catapult through
the gaps between bars
when emotions get the better.

It's bruised from trying but healing in stages,
blue plumming up to bloodred, slow.
Skinner's box is a cold hug.
Elusive pellet: be mine,
for good job done or lesson learned
something, anything
I can grasp with these tired
thumbs.

clog: a series

* * *

A tumor is an abnormal mass of cells which can be either
malignant (cancerous) or benign (noncancerous). Although
benign tumors only grow locally, they can still be dangerous
or disfiguring and may be surgically removed.

He is the skeleton in your cloakroom, Clog
the black sheep in your family
the one your aunts never bring up
over coffee + lemon slice

> *I wonder what he's up to now*
>
> *where's he livin'*
> *these days?*

He is lost on their tongues
from their minds, but he is there
            a photo crammed between
calendars + wrapping paper
his sticky fingerprints
stained on the pages of your favorite
book, if you close your eyes
+ breathe
you can smell him

* * *

In malignant tumors, the cells replicate uncontrollably,
and quickly. Malignant cells can also spread to other parts
of the body, which is called metastasis (me-TAS-ta-sis).

He is horny, Clog
+ he is his own master
getting himself up
during dry spells
hot breath beer
grunts calluses on soft
flesh, hard staring at
the bath mat

that   needs   a

           wash

                  ohgod needs

ah

Clog sows his oats, too
+ plenty of them,
gives new meaning
to the word dead/
beat   the patter of a
thousand perfect shadows
in his wake

* * *

The process of metastasis begins with malignant cells invading the neighbouring tissues. The growing cancer competes with normal tissues for space and nutrients. This growth is continuous and progressive, ending in the destruction of the normal tissues.

He's confused, Clog
just can't figure it out
how he parachutes in
at Christmas, fat clay ass
planted on the couch
for weeks, eating + never
giving in or getting up
shoving in porkhocks drumsticks
plumpudding thimble cookies
chocolate cherries
(the kind that dribble juice through
candy-cracks + down his chins)

gotta breathe gotta   breathe

He can be persuaded to leave though
horkin' side of beef
dangling on a hook
a bowl of au jus +
Yorkshire pudding the size
of a blimp cruising
                        out the door

* * *

*Following invasion, some of the malignant cells may break
away from the main tumor and grow in nearby areas such as the
abdominal cavity or enter the bloodstream or lymphatic system.
This can lead to widespread metastasis, the next step.*

He is rough + tumble, Clog
+ angry   drifting
along twisted city streets
+ arteries
blown into
town, stumbling
     on a quest for love
drunk + stinking
through his pores
drooling through
his tongue
eyes like marbles
hitting the sun
his hands hitting
everything they can
it's all he knows

he knows

* * *

The cells travel to a distant site in the body and colonize.
Pain develops when the cancerous growth presses on organs,
nerves or bones or blocks a passageway causing secretions
to build up pressure.

He is BoneDaddy, Clog
not so sweet as
sugar, coaxing them
one by one to
take him in
to put him up
He would give them
the world (just
wouldn't say which)
while oysters drunk
+ swollen slide
down throats at Earls:

if you touch me

  i will

      make

          you

   dance

By morning, his search
is on again
an empty bed
the only clue
they're bags of bones
in the corner
his stench tattooed
in their pores

losing our marbles

We were losing our marbles.
But always finding more, stored
in the deep, purple-felt pockets
of Crown Royal bags
starkly repurposed
to hold a child's currency.

Our kindergarten stock market
saw power change hands
in peewees + jumbo crocks.
Each commodity unique
+ valued accordingly,
our portfolios diversified
in a rainforest of orbs:

>   glass globes injected
>   with ribbons preserved   mid-twirl
>   realistic + mysterious
>   as jarred pimentos;

>   solid ceramics,
>   surfaces pepperminted like circus tents
>   or dropped into backdrafts,
>   licked in flames;

>   + Tiger's Eyes
>   plucked straight from
>   amber sockets,
>   still glaring.

There, on that grassy backyard trading floor—
our version of Bay St.—
we cut our teeth on economic concepts,
rode the teeter-totter forces
of supply + demand   floating

>   + falling

as the unblinking prairie sun
baked our shiny wagers
into deals.

We greased the small palms
of friends for first dibs,
learning early the art of barter,
how to propagate need.   Then dreamed

of launching our collections beyond
suburban borders to whet
the relentless appetite of global masses
clucking for *more, more, more.*

We were losing our marbles, alright,
with our childhoods   sliding ladderless
down a snakepit of a hole
our wide-eyed minds couldn't realize
was never-ending:

      We'll always need
      more product to move. Also, bodies.

      We'll always need more bodies
      to stay in this game.

u-pick strawberry farm

The sun skimmed early fog off open fields
each dewy peel revealing
a scrubbed iteration: row upon row
of blood-coloured chubs, luscious
on the vine.

Yesterday's abortion took
+ her womb clammed + clammed for hours
finishing up the business. Cramps came on
like a civic uprising + nothing
could quell that tide of discontent
but the ticking minutes,

a bomb in reverse.

Today's agenda: finding catharsis in harvest,
liberating berries in their prime,
sour-sweet buzz of these virtuous bursts
surprising the tongue.

She fingers the earth for assurances
scouring for signs in the cycles
for evidence that miracles
will eventually recur
if conditions become
anywhere nearer
to ideal.

dear uterus

fist-of-cuffs
fist of blood
more often clenched
in suspense   + suspended

red-brained lady-in-waiting
swollen plum
with its skin slipped off
self-cleaning (if temperamental)
easy-bake oven

hardscrabble battler,
grinder with abundant pluck
you run amok,
calling the shots but rarely getting
what you want:

baby this, *baby* that

this obsession of yours borders
on ridiculous

endometriosis

Doctor: my back throbs
every morning a sandbag
on my kidneys   my belly gorged
like it's busting with a fist of life,
but moon after moon
the dream recedes in low tide.

Ultrasound shows a *chocolate cyst*
which sounds almost delicious
if it weren't filled
with my own old blood,
a disgusting truffle.

Months pass before I'm split
open for the reveal:
a dusty landscape studded
with *gunpowder burns*.

My insides are a Wild West showdown,
a saloon bristling with disgruntled patrons
their cracked-glass highballs rippling with
whisky, cactus wine, tanglefoot.
The rusted doors of my cervix creak.

The surgeon wields her own weapon,
sizzles off scar tissue, cuts other junk away:
tube stalks, *adhesions* in the cul-de-sac,
the perineum. My bloody truffle.

It's everywhere.

She's my hifalutin' hero, runs the blue dye test.
My bowel is, thankfully, intact.

* * *

Cleansed, I'm wheeled to recovery
in an avocado recliner.
Now I'm the flying nun
donning a habit of hot blankets
to exorcise the chill. I haunt
the Victorian halls of St. Joseph's
+ see the truth:

> that the scar will never absolve
> nor resolve
> nor rewind to virgin

is a perennial new abuse
perpetually fresh
+ unrepentant
forever + ever
+ ever

amen.

my pelvis

a rainforest
bloated with old growth
+ smoking bulletholes

one day we raze the land
but cannot stop the grass
from being grass

sickbed

In the misery of illness
I regret that I haven't been kinder
to those around me, more compassionate
toward their lack of patience
for how easy could it be
to empty my endless bedpan
of complaints?

The metaphors have arrived,
feathering the bedroom ceiling
with clever projections of my demise,
begin to pick at my skin
starting with leftover moles
the surgeons didn't steal years before.
They must prefer my scant dark meat;
what I lack in melanin
I make up for in melancholy.
These days I'm a real hoot.

Now I call my sickbed *home*
+ hang my sweaty dreams to dry.
From the boulevard, the maple tree waggles
its cheeky green tongues at me.
Ah, the chartreuse of youth.
Joy in taking for granted, good health
the silent *bingo!*
everybody forgets
to yell.

weaning off antidepressant, early days

someone call the fuzz

                                          a conundrum is coming

      is coming down

                                   coming

                                              down

              down

has landed

rolling brownouts: intermittent fizz of lights
like cigarette drags, electrical surges
fry brainmeat in its pot of bone
nerves are scalped, even shadows
cause the skin to chicken   muscles screech

+ when the head turns
the eyes take three seconds to catch up
like a live-tv censor delay
but in real-time
the body sweats its full weight
into the sheets

relieved of a lifeline
borders become frayed
rulebook abandoned
the mind has no plan
for how to behave

nostalgic
for the doldrum days

mercurybomb

Bored
my sister + I once cracked
a glass thermometer in half, watched
its bloodball burst + the quicksilver spill out the shaft
    shimmering +
            cleaving
      into reproductions
of itself   like funhouse mirrors giving birth
+ exiting a clown car.

For hours
we watched this uncommitted
straddler of states   shatter
      + shapeshift   as it pinballed across the headboard

as it slinkied the staircase we made
with our hands, dropping

      down
            down

      down

like the Tin Man's
tears.

What cellular chaos
was spawned that day   in our toxic play
while the eyes in the back of our mother's head
expired?

     DNA rearranged into 70s plaid
         or permanently edited fingerprints?

What chemical aftermath   decades in the making
might some day trigger little missiles to multiply
             rippling

      + glittering like

                         jumping

        fish in our autumn

riverveins?

These days I feel fine   though
compelled to regular checkups   so I slip

the cool slim rod
    under my tongue
               + wait

                      wait

                wait
for that bloodshot
to rise.

pomegranate seeds

O glossy bullets
between my teeth, you deliver

your message of hope
in explosions. Popped

balloons surprising
the tongue with your cold

carnage, spatter-patterns
on the cheek-

meat. Like Trojan horses
once inside, your red

army gets to work
jewel boots on the ground.

notes on the poems

"Don Music" was a *Sesame Street*™ character—an agonized composer who took out his songwriting frustrations on his piano...and his head.

The quote introducing "the buzzer" is from a *National Post* article published on May 13, 2019.

"Allow the face to speak in its natural idiom." is taken from *The Elements of Typographic Style* by Robert Bringhurst.

acknowledgements

My deepest gratitude to NeWest Press: Matt Bowes and the editorial committee for enabling this incredible ride; Douglas Barbour for his steady encouragement and editor's sharp eye; Claire Kelly for her guidance and insightful analysis. And to Natalie Olsen at Kisscut Design for expertly, and deliciously, bringing it all to life.

A number of poems have appeared or are forthcoming in the following publications: *Another Dysfunctional Cancer Poem Anthology, CAROUSEL, FreeFall, untethered, Room, Prairie Fire* and *Contemporary Verse 2*. I'm grateful to those editors for giving my work a first home.

This collection began many years ago, so I thank my creative writing instructor and mentor, Patrick Friesen, whose contagious passion sparked my love for poetry and the boundless possibilities of language. I'm enormously indebted to Karen Connelly, my editor at the Humber School for Writers and beyond. Her wisdom, encouragement, kindness and humour lit my way.

Thanks-times-infinity to my parents, Norma and Len Harvey, for their steadfast support of all my pursuits and for fostering my creative spirit from the start. And to my dear in-laws, Jane and Wayne Steski, for allowing me precious time and space to work and also for providing the inspirational settings in several of the poems.

I am lucky to have a team of enthusiastic cheerleaders by my side. Love to my family and friends who have supported me along the way: Alison, Don, Mackenzie, Brigit and Jake Harvey; Janet Harvey and Blair Wankling; Peter Steski; Kimberly, John, Rhianna, Jack and Emmalena Steski; Natalie Swanson; Cheryl Kehler; Kristen Martin; Orla and Don Douglas; Jodi and Jon Finkelstein; and Sofia Johan and Douglas Cumming. Numerous work colleagues, whom I consider friends, have also lifted me up through the years.

And a special shout out to Valerie Fish and Jennifer Kjell for their professional advice. It has been a lifeline.

To Jeff, my best friend, thank you for believing in me and for helping me chase my passion. Also, for keeping our home organized ("If it's not a *right* angle, it's a *wrong* angle." LOL) and happy. To Anya, my inspiration, you are my best dream come true. I love you, little family. xo

In 2017, to honour NeWest Press' 40th anniversary, we inaugurated a new poetry series to go alongside our Nunatak First Fiction, Prairie Play, and Writer as Critic series: Crow Said Poetry. Crow Said is named in honour of Robert Kroetsch's foundational 1977 novel *What The Crow Said*. The series aims to shed light on places and people outside of the literary mainstream. It is our intention that the poets featured in this series will continue Robert Kroetsch's literary tradition of innovation, interrogation, and generosity of spirit.

CROW SAID POETRY TITLES AVAILABLE FROM NEWEST

Tar Swan — David Martin

That Light Feeling Under Your Feet — Kayla Geitzler

Paper Caskets — Emilia Danielewska

let us not think of them as barbarians — Peter Midgley

Lullabies in the Real World — Meredith Quartermain

The Response of Weeds: A Misplacement of Black Poetry on the Prairies — Bertrand Bickersteth

Coconut — Nisha Patel

rump + flank — Carol Harvey Steski

Carol Harvey Steski grew up under the wide Winnipeg sky. Her poems have been published in the poetry anthology *Another Dysfunctional Cancer Poem Anthology*, and literary magazines including *Room*, *Prairie Fire*, *FreeFall*, *untethered*, *Contemporary Verse 2,* and *CAROUSEL*. Her work was featured in Winnipeg Transit's "Poetry in Motion" program and tootled around town on buses. Twice she was a finalist in *FreeFall*'s annual poetry contest. As a young-adult survivor of melanoma she has been a guest on CBC Radio-Manitoba speaking about the therapeutic benefits of writing through disease. She lives in Toronto with her husband and daughter, working in corporate communications. *rump + flank* is her debut poetry collection. Visit her website: **carolharveysteski.com**. Connect with her on Twitter: **@charveysteski** and Instagram: **@carolharveysteski**.